Cof Gwyntor

Cornetti

The Chronicles of Gwynfor Cornetti

Ian Ashton

y Lolfa

First impression: 2013

© Copyright Ian Ashton and Y Lolfa Cyf., 2013

Cover illustration: Huw Aaron
Cover design: Y Lolfa

ISBN: 978 184771 639 2

FSC

Published and printed in Wales
on paper from well maintained forests by
Y Lolfa Cyf., Talybont, Ceredigion SY24 5HE
website www.ylolfa.com
e-mail ylolfa@ylolfa.com
tel 01970 832 304
fax 832 782

Contents

Poems

Stories

Gwynfor Cornetti

Gwynfor Cornetti who lives in Penarth
One Saturday evening was sat in his bath,
Removing his corns with a bit of old tufa
And singing 'Delilah' into his loofah.

He lay on his back and he watched in a dream
The window where runnels condensed from the steam.
As each drop of water descended the pane
Gwynfor Cornetti observed them again.

They twisted and turned and to Gwynfor's surprise
They etched out a picture in front of his eyes.
He leaped from the bath and 'eureka' he said,
"A wonderful thought has come into my head.

"If water is steam and then steam turns to water
There must be a moment when they have to alter,
And no more be water yet neither be steam.
I have the idea for a wonderful scheme.

"I'll look for the moment in time and in space
When water's state alters and then I can trace
The instant in time when time's become static
And all that surrounds it in time is erratic."

So he went to his shed and worked for a week
On making a time machine so he could peek
At time in its essence so that people could see
Things that had happened and things that would be.

With prisms and switches and cathodes and clocks
And some pure copper coils he'd nicked from the docks,
He joined them together and put them in order
With a telescope, lens and an ancient camcorder.

He had worked out before where the prisms would go
And switches and lens, so the whole thing would show
The events of the past and what yet never had been
As clear as you like on a fourteen-inch screen.

And when it was finished he called *Wedi Saith**
And the producer invited Gwynfor and his wife
To appear on the programme for the nation to view
The first time machine of which anyone knew.

The following night the reporter came round
And she checked them for light and she checked them for sound
And they waited for seven o'clock to arrive
When the nation would see the first time machine live.

The reporter explained what they all had to do
And on thousands of tellies there sprang into view
The girl telling everyone Gwynfor's machine
Could now capture time to display on a screen.

They went back in time and saw people long dead,
Saint David, Saint Illtyd and Eric the Red,
Who no one had known 'til the screen made it clear,
Had been in Penarth when the Vikings were here.

The machine only showed what had happened nearby
And as time was short Gwynfor said he would try
To look for some things that were more up-to-date
And altered the dial to nineteen-o-eight.

There was his granny when she was a girl
And after he'd given the knob one more twirl
Everyone watching the programme then saw
The Luftwaffe bombing Penarth in the war.

He twiddled the knob once again and the screen
Changed to another more up-to-date scene.
And Gwynfor announced, "it would seem we arrive
At yesterday fortnight at quarter to five."

The view was the same room as they were now in
But the scene on the screen was of cardinal sin.
And the audience watching at home plainly saw
His wife making love to the man from next door!

*   Live magazine programme (now called *Heno*) on S4C at
    19:00 hrs. Much recommended.

Dai Cynwal's imaginary friend

When Dai Cynwal was just a boy he had a special friend,
Another boy, a bit like him, but he was just pretend.
Dai's playmate didn't steal his sweets, and didn't break Dai's toys
Nor beat him up for nothing as did all the other boys.
He didn't snitch or split on Dai, and always told the truth,
Nor get Dai into trouble – not this paragon of youth.
He never varied in his ways and knew no aberration
That noble, upright figment of Dai's young imagination.
But even though Dai thought him up, his playmate acted sly.
Just like all the other children he refused to play with Dai.

Eleri Marion Twysog-Hughes

Eleri Marion Twysog-Hughes
Went to buy herself some shoes.
But on her way to the shops in Llysweri
Some aliens came and abducted Eleri.

It wasn't long on their trip through space
They regretted their deed, that alien race.
And they brought her back at the speed of light
To the place where they'd found her, the following night.

For she nagged and scolded the alien crew
In the way that girls called Eleri do.
She made them polish and scrub and clean
Every part of their space machine.

And she chided the captain for being green
And stamped her foot and created a scene
When she found some ray guns not in their rack
And made all the aliens put them back.

And when the aliens sat to lunch
She made them wash and told the bunch
To eat their meal in perfect quiet,
And put two-thirds of them on a diet.

And she made the aliens disembogue
Their gin – and their pictures of Kylie Minogue
She confiscated as being too lewd,
She wanted the ship more virtuously crewed.

And she nagged and bullied 'til the crew all swore
They didn't think they could stand any more.
And they told the captain they thought it best
To go back down to earth with their guest.

For the thought of the trip back home as planned
With Eleri was more than the crew could stand.
So they took her back and put her down
In the selfsame spot where she'd been in town.

For the aliens thought that it wasn't worth
The trouble she'd given to conquer Earth.
And they thought in the end that they wouldn't choose
To share a planet with Mrs Hughes.

But when her husband Morgan learned
That the crew of the alien craft had spurned
The chance to take his wife away
He hanged himself the following day.

Menna and the daffodil

Menna Owen and her corgi went out for a walk.
And Menna found a daffodil called Blodwyn who could talk.
The daffodil was most polite and went on to explain
That Blodwyn was a pseudonym and not her proper name.
The flower said the reason she'd decided to renounce
Her flower name – was humans found it too hard to pronounce.
And Blodwyn's such a pretty name she thought that it might bring
A touch of something pleasant into Cathay's Park each spring.
And Menna said that daffodils were such a pleasant sight
And Blodwyn said that Menna was exceedingly polite.
And Menna and the daffodil stood chatting there for hours
As if there's nothing strange at all in talking to the flowers.
The corgi sniffed around the plant and tried to dig it out
Then cocked its leg and wee'd on it and got a hefty clout
From Menna for its trouble and it yelped and ran away
And killed a rat to vent its spleen, and Menna had to say
Sorry to the daffodil who said she didn't mind
Because that sort of thing was just accepted by her kind.
"It happens fairly regular, one gets trampled on and kicked,"
The plant explained, "and sometimes one gets sat upon or picked."
"There's not a lot that one can do about the fact my dear,"
The daffodil told Menna, "but to grow again next year."
And Menna asked the daffodil if she would not prefer
If Menna put her in a pot and took her home with her.
The daffodil was overjoyed, accepting right away,
And Menna dug her up and took her home without delay.

The park attendant stopped her at the gate before she left
And asked her if she realized she'd committed petty theft.
But when the flower spoke to him his chin was on the floor
And secretly he vowed to not go drinking anymore.
As soon as he was on his own he sneaked behind the hedge
And poured his cache of gin away and went and signed the pledge.
In Menna's house in Radyr there's a terracotta pot
On her chintzy kitchen window sill and in it she has got
Some multi-purpose compost and some dried fish, blood and bone
That's a little bit of Wales a daffodil can call it's own.
And every year in springtime Blodwyn blossoms into bloom
And the happy sound of chatter permeates throughout the room.
And the daffodil and Menna have got such a lot to say
'Til the second week in April when her flower fades away
And Blodwyn withers down until her bulb is all that's left,
And the kitchen falls to silence and poor Menna feels bereft
Of her only bit of company, and the only friend she's got,
Besides her little corgi, who's now silent in her pot.
So she puts some Baby Bio on the compost for her friend
And moves her to a shady spot determined she will tend
To all her little needs and wants throughout the coming year
Until it's early spring again when green shoots will appear,
And Blodwyn will come back again and brighten up the room
And in Menna Owen's kitchen all the chatter can resume.

The Tale of Meredith Prosser

Poor Meredith Prosser was only ten stone,
Not very much more than some freckles and bone,
Some wispy fair hair and a layer of skin
That his mother had given him to wrap himself in.
He talked with a lisp and he walked with a stoop,
He had halitosis and suffered from croup.
He was bandy and pimpled and had one of those faces
That looks like it's lost all it had at the races.
And the love of his life was his friend's sister Megan
A spotty young beanpole from Abergwyngregan.
He followed her round like a puppy on heat.
And she cut him dead if they met on the street.
He went to his friend and said, "what shall I do?"
His friend looked at him and said, "if I was you
I'd say bother with Megan and look for another.
But then maybe I'm biased because I'm her brother."
But Meredith knew that that wasn't for him –
His love wasn't based on a pubescent whim.
He was seventeen then and he'd loved her for years,
He was rather more constant than most of his peers.
He had to have Megan, it wasn't just lust,
For Meredith it was his Megan or bust.
So he begged that his friend would explain like a pal
What he had to achieve to make Megan his gal.
"It's like this," said her brother, "though I don't like to say

You'd have more chance with Megan if Megan was gay
Than you do as you are. Megan thinks you're too thin.
Get some muscles for Megan and then you'll be in."
That was it for young Prosser, he went there and then
On a run to Llanberis and straight back again.
He did press-ups and sit-ups and squat thrusts with vigour,
But his biceps and pectorals didn't get any bigger.
And after a fortnight he still was too slim,
So he went into Bangor and booked in the gym.
There they'd dumbbells and barbells and punch-bags and stuff
Which he lifted and thumped 'til he ran out of puff.
By the end of the month he had proved their best scholar
But still couldn't fill out a fourteen-inch collar.
The gym was so sorry because of his lack
Of muscles they gave him his fifty quid back.
And Meredith went on the bus to Benllech
To jump in the sea with a rock round his neck.
But he came back again from the beach in disgrace
Because two little girls had kicked sand in his face.
He sat on a bench on the edge of the sands
With his heart in his boots and his head in his hands
When a page from the *Afon Wen Bugle* blew by
With a quarter page advert that captured his eye.
It carried a picture of someone so slim
And so weedy that Meredith thought it was him.
But Meredith saw with his very own eyes
That thirty days later he'd trebled in size.
For a man in the picture, Mr Mighty by name,
Was there underneath in the very next frame.
The advert said send a cash warrant to me

For eighty-six pounds and I will guarantee
If you do all the things that I say in my book
Then this is the way that you're going to look.
Now Meredith started by doing his sums
And by using his fingers and both of his thumbs
He found he could muster the eighty-six quid
So he went back to Bangor and that's what he did.
And he sent off his cheque to the place in the ad,
And he never considered for once he'd been had.
And he waited, and waited and waited some more
For a parcel he'd paid for to drop through the door.
He grew thinner and thinner with each passing day
Until in the end he just wasted away.
It wasn't that long after he was no more
That Megan had married his neighbour next door,
A boy who until he was nearly eighteen
Was more skinny than Meredith ever had been,
But who suddenly changed to gargantuan size
With huge, mighty muscles and thunderous thighs
And a forty-eight chest and thirty-two waist.
A transfiguration his mother had traced
To a book he'd been given by the Prossers next door
Who had told him their son wouldn't need it no more
On account it arrived on the very next day
After the son that they'd loved passed away.
And because in their grief they had thought it was better
To give him the book and not open the letter
They had not seen the note that explained the delay,
Was because there was postage and packing to pay.
The note was quite nice and went on to explain

It was there in the advert, which made it quite plain.
But their boss, Mr Mighty said that he understood
And he hoped that the course would do Meredith good.
And as Mr Mighty was such a nice man
Meredith can pay it as soon as he can.

Thomas Jenkins
and the Krakken

Thomas Jenkins shooting stones was quite surprised to hear
A voice shout "oi" and find his stone come whizzing past his ear.
He took his trusty catapult and shot another stone
And heard a shout of "oi" again and thought, "I'm not alone."
He shot another pebble out towards the selfsame place
Across the Bristol Channel, and it skimmed back at his face.
It hit him on the shoulder and made it very sore,
A thing that Thomas Jenkins hadn't come across before.
He scrutinized around himself and after taking stock,
He searched around among the stones and took another rock
Which he shot across the water, as he had the other three
And that came skimming back as well and hit him on the knee.
So he limped down to the water's edge and wondered what in heaven
Was out there in the Channel as he peered across to Devon.
He picked up half a dozen stones and shot them one by one
And every stone came flying back just as the first had done.
"Is anybody out there, look?" Thomas Jenkins said.
And from the murky, muddy depths, there rose a reptile's head.
The head was thirty-eight feet long and yellow underneath
But green on top and had a mouth with nineteen-inch long teeth.
"There's me," the Krakken told him, "I'm the Krakken don't
    you know.
And I object to idiots who come along and throw
Great boulders in the Channel where I've settled for a rest

For a moment from my wanderings, you thoughtless little pest."
"I didn't know that Krakkens came to Wentlooge as a rule,"
Said Thomas, "they don't teach about the Krakkens in our school.
We only do humanities and modern history
And how to empathize with everybody that we see.
What Krakkens do and where they live and what they are for sure
Are things one doesn't know not having heard of them before."
"The first thing that you have to know," the Krakken told the lad
"Is I'm the only Krakken, and I think it's very bad
That modern education doesn't tell you of my kind.
I really should be better known about, and have in mind
A little demonstration that will bring me to the fore
With all those folk you say have never heard of me before.
I will cause a major tidal wave to flood the coast of Devon
And all the land on either side that borders on the Severn.
I'll have to take a run at it, and swim out past the Gower,
Then come back in behind the tide at ninety miles an hour.
But if I get my timing right, and I'm careful how I do it,
I will drive a wall of water ten feet high up past Portskewett."
"That really isn't very nice," young Thomas Jenkins said.
"Just think of all the people who are going to end up dead."
"I know," the Krakken answered with the coldness of his kind.
"I don't suppose they'll like it. Dear, how sad, but never mind.
At least the ones who haven't drowned aren't likely to forget
Just who and what the Krakken is, or what he's called I bet."
Then he turned round in the water and Thomas Jenkins saw
His head was furlongs distant while his tail was on the shore.
Then he swam off down the Channel, and he came back on the tide,
Behind a wave he'd made that stretched right to the English side.
But as he shot past Wentlooge like a clipper in full sail
Thomas Jenkins tied his catapult around the Krakken's tail

And he wedged the wooden handle round a boulder on the beach
And watched to see how far the catapult would let him reach.
He reckoned that the Krakken must have reached the end of Gwent
When suddenly it shot back past, much faster than it went.
It flew downstream past Flat Holm then rebounded back again
All the way back up the river mouth, until it felt the strain
Of the catapult elastic pull him down the estuary
Past Summerleaze and Goldcliff and past Wentlooge back to sea.
And the Krakken bounces up and down the river to this day
On the end of his elastic and I've heard some people say
That when the tide is right and when the Krakken's near the shore
The wave the Krakken pushes up will cause the Severn Bore.

Y Brodyr Brynsiencyn

Two brothers from Brynsiencyn had bickered all their lives
They bickered with their neighbours and they bickered with
    their wives.
The bickered for a hobby. They bickered day and night.
And when they were not bickering they'd stop and have a fight.

They bickered over horses and they bickered over hay.
They never stopped for anything and bickered every day.
One day they went out ploughing and at noon they sat to rest,
And they bickered with each other as to who could plough the best.

They bickered for a fortnight, each one making it his boast
That however and whenever he would always plough the most.
So they said they'd have a contest and they started out next day
With a team of ploughing oxen up and down to Colwyn Bay.

Back and forth they went past Bangor, always ploughing side by side
Each one matching with the other, pull for pull and stride for stride.
Where the Seiont met the ocean they would turn their teams around
And not stopping for a breather they would both be Conwy-bound.

After getting to Llandudno they would see their team got fed
And the spoil kicked up in turning helped to form the Great
    Orme's Head.
Then they'd head back to Caernarvon, never breaking in their stride
'Til the furrows they were ploughing grew to be a mile wide.

And they kept on for a twelvemonth, neither one would give
    the other
Any latitude or leeway, even though he was his brother.
Except, of course, on Sundays, when they took their Sabbath rest,
In the choir in Caernarvon where they bickered who was best.

Then one Sabbath the two brothers, who had rested from
    their labour,
And were bickering about a bit of grazing with a neighbour,
Heard the sound of rushing water, like a mighty torrent's roar
And the brothers looked with horror from each other to the door.

Then the chapel congregation went and had a look outside
Where they saw a band of water that was half a mile wide.
It ran all the way past Bangor, and the brothers had to note
That to get back to Brynsiencyn they would have to buy a boat.

It was plain to everybody that the furrow they had ploughed
Was too deep an excavation and the pair had not allowed
For the shoring that was needed at the seaward end to be
In a suitable condition to keep out the Irish Sea.

And that's the way that Anglesey, or Ynys Môn, was made
And no person in Caernarfon is in anyway dismayed
That the people from Brynsiencyn and Llangaffo to this date
Have been separated from them by the tidal Menai Strait.

Pysgotwr Cas-gwent*

I am the Chepstow fisherman
I'm manly, rough and tough.
To shows how rough and tough I am
I fishes in the buff.

The mudflats of the Severn
Is where the west wind blows
And where I plies my heritage
Devoid of any clothes.

The icy blasts from Gloucestershire
Are cutting, cold and keen,
As are the winds from Somerset,
And those from off the Dean.

The waters of the River Wye,
Which we use to anoint
Our bodies, seldom elevate
A lot past freezing point.

And yet we Chepstow fishermen
You'll notice, have eschewed,
Our clothes when we go fishing.
We does do it in the nude.

We do not care for rubber boots,
Nor scarf, nor knitted hat,
Nor woolly combinations,
Nor not anything like that.

We fishes in our birthday suits,
No matter what the weather.
We finds it more efficient
Fishing in the altogether.

They should make a statue of us
That is bronzed and tanned and ruddy
Which we be when we fishes
In the Severn, in the nuddy.

Believe this affirmation,
Fishermen don't lie.
We always fishes in the nude,
It helps the pigs to fly.

*Upon the unveiling of 'The Fisherman' statue in Chepstow

A cautionary tale
of an unwise marriage

Since Wynford Jones got married he's been prone to introspection
As far as he can tell his wife's devoid of a reflection.
In their bedroom on their honeymoon was when he noticed first,
And what he's noticed ever since has gone from bad to worst.
He watched her in the mirror sitting down to brush her hair
And tried to catch her eye but her reflection wasn't there.
When the wedding photographs came back he claims that on his life
There was no trace of anyone connected to his wife.
In every photo of them both his wife just isn't there
And he's left looking foolish, leaning over kissing air.
And when his dog first saw his wife it slunk off backwards growling
And now at night it alternates twixt whimpering and howling.
His sister called his wife a bitch the morning they were wed,
It's strange a girl so full of health should suddenly drop dead.
Her relatives will only come at night-times when they visit,
And always leave before the dawn. That isn't normal is it?
And Muriel, his wife that is, so far as he can judge,
Spends all day in the cellar, out from whence she doesn't budge.
She claims she does her research work, but he has never heard,
Of research done in coffins, but still he takes her word.
But when she does her research work he can't see why she must
Conduct her research covered in some foreign looking dust.
Their love life isn't up to much, they seldom misbehave,
Unless she finds he's cut himself when Wynford's had a shave.

That seems to turn her on and make her slightly less remote.
Though while they're making love she's mostly nibbling his throat.
The house that they have rented from her uncle's not a home,
It's full of doleful voices, even when they're both alone.
Now matter how the Aga burns, he never finds it warm,
And outside there's a permanent and massive thunderstorm.
He cannot hear the telly for the noise of constant shrieking,
The doors keep flying open and the floorboards keep on creaking,
And on the kitchen skirting board there is a nasty stain
Which, if he cleans it off, comes back next morning once again,
His wife considers all these things which he finds strange,
    quite normal
And yet insists their dinner dress is never less than formal.
He cannot chase the rats away, despite the germs they harbour,
Nor clean the dust and cobwebs that festoon the candelabra.
He doesn't drink the wine she drinks, he has his own instead,
He's never seen wine quite that thick, nor quite that shade of red,
The way it bubbles in the glass is nothing short of Hellish,
He hates it how, when drinking it, she stares at him with relish.
The butler's not his cup of tea, and he has never seen
A butler quite as tall as him, nor quite that shade of green.
One night he said, "I'm leaving. I'll be seeking a divorce."
The butler said he couldn't go and kept him there by force.
He told him how the 'Mistress' had expressly made it plain
That he must stop him leaving and was free to cause him pain.
When Wynford said, "I've got to leave. To keep me here is wrong."
The butler said, "Don't worry sir. You won't be staying long."
And then explained, and blanched a bit, beneath his sickly sheen,
He'd never known a 'Master' linger much past Halloween.

Ad Astra Per Ardua

Somewhere not far from Rhiwbina
They're planning to conquer the stars
By building a steam-powered spaceship
To land the first Welshman on Mars.

They've built it in Dan Watkin's garden
But they daren't tell his partner the truth.
She thinks they're extending her kitchen
And the nose cone's a bit of the roof.

The cockpit sticks out of the Tŷ Bach,*
So the pilot climbs up by a ladder.
And the boiler has come from a loco
They've scrounged from the goods' yard in Radyr.

The whole thing's a bit of a secret,
The project's been going for years
At weekends and late in the evening,
In case NASA should pinch their ideas.

They applied for a grant for the budget.
The Assembly's been given the cost,
But they're having to wait for an answer.
It appears their submission's been lost.

Dai Evans is going to fly it.
He goes into training next week,
On a diet of curry and press-ups
To give him the perfect physique.

The fuel will be fed from a hopper
So the pilot can work the controls
Without having to stop what he's doing
To constantly shovel the coals.

The steam will go through a condenser,
By way of a bleed tap, you see
To save Dai from boiling a kettle
When he fancies a nice cup of tea.

The launch is a fortnight on Friday
They can put it back for one day,
But it has to be that day or never,
Because Cardiff are playing away.

So if you're in Whitchurch that Friday,
Make sure that you wish them good luck,
And if you are out in Caerphilly,
Be perfectly ready to duck.

* Tŷ Bach: Lit. "little house", the outside toilet

The Cassowary

It's little known the cassowary used to live just south of Barry
In a sort of ratite heaven, before the waters of the Severn
Grew much wider than intended when the last great Ice Age ended.
So the cassowary had to roam and find himself another home,
Where the weather is much hotter, still you find he thinks a lotta
'Bout the time when he could freely go from Penarth to
     Westward Ho.

The cockle

You will find the hardy cockle,
From Ynys-las to distant Rockall.
Such a varied distribution,
Bespeaks its hardy constitution.

The foolish pigeon from Trenewydd Park, Risca

A pigeon from Trenewydd Park
Decided one day, for a lark,
To fly to Porthcawl
With no thought at all
For how he'd get back in the dark.

The Great Bard
of Llanfair-Discoed

She struggled hard for many years to teach herself to read
Though all her friends and half he peers opined there was no need.
They couldn't see the reason why she should acquire the skill.
There were a few who thought her mad, and some who thought
    her ill.
They told her, "all we ever do is eat and drink and sleep.
Why not just be illiterate like any other sheep?"
But she was most determined that was what she had to do.
Indeed she was quite different from every other ewe.
She made her mind up years ago and studied every night
And once she'd taught herself to read, she taught herself to write.
She wrote to the Eisteddfod telling them she'd like to be
The first Welsh Mountain ewe to win the chair for poetry.
She sent a sample of her work, a *cywydd* she'd composed
Which really was much better than the Gorsedd had supposed.
And so they wrote back to the sheep and said they wanted proof
The work was hers and so she made an imprint of her hoof
Upon an affidavit her solicitor had signed
Which was the sort of guarantee the Gorsedd had in mind.
They took the entry from the sheep and judged it with the rest
Without a hint of prejudice to see which was the best.
She didn't win the chair of course, that would have been absurd.
But she was fairly happy when they said she'd come in third.
The great archdruid, later, in the bar was heard to state

He rather liked the work he'd heard done by the ungulate.
And all the bards and judges said they didn't think to find
A sheep at the Eisteddfod who had got a first-rate mind.
So she went to university and she is thought to be
The only quadruped to have a second-class degree.
Her tutors thought she'd get a first, but she was quite content,
And after graduation made her way back home to Gwent.
And now she lives in Caldicot and calls herself Annette
And writes a weekly column in the *Pontypool Gazette.*

The Gulls of the Gower

Above the rocks of Bracelet Bay
The seagulls circle night and day.
Left to right they go at night.
From dawn they go the other way.

But on the Gower's other side
The seagulls which by there reside
Go in and out, not roundabout
With the ever changing tide.

The Maid from Pontypool

In Pontypool there lived a maid whose wedding had to be delayed
Because the wedding dress she'd bought had grown a weenie bit
     too taut
Between the bodice and the hip because she'd made a little slip.
A slip that she found rather nice but contravened her ma's advice.
Never mind, although she's grown a trifle large, she's not alone,
And on her wedding night there'll be a bit of extra company.
Her spouse-to-be thinks what's inside the swelling stomach of
     his bride
Is his and thus is bound to be his own responsibility.
And as he's come to that conclusion she will not shatter his illusion,
A circumstance that's not at all unique to her in Pontypool.

The Nun's Tale

Not far from Bont in Monmouthshire
The convent stands alone
Its ancient walls festooned with moss
And gardens overgrown.

The order of the Sacred Heart
Maintains its cloistered ways
As it has done for centuries
Since medieval days.

Eight sisters in their seventies
Keep vigil night and day
In silence and in solitude
Processing as they pray.

One prioress who leads them all
Is older than the eight.
And there's another younger nun
In her noviciate.

They do not speak except to pray,
They are a silent order,
That has renounced all earthly things
Beside the English border.

The acolyte who joined their ranks
Is only twenty-one
And working hard to take her vows
And be a proper nun.

She seldom leaves her tiny cell
And everybody says
They've never known a novice nun
So thorough in her ways.

They hear her tell her rosary
For hours through the night
Which fills their honest eyes with tears
And hearts with pure delight.

But what the nuns don't realize
The old chants of their order
They think the novice sings at night
Are on a tape recorder.

For being younger than the rest
She's fitter and much stronger
Than all the other aged nuns
Who have been nuns much longer.

And so she does the heavy work
And works the garden plot
And tends the massive greenhouse where
The novice grows her pot.

She also cleans the chantry hall,
On top of Hatterfall Hill,
Where all the older nuns can't go,
And there she has a still.

And she has dug a tunnel
From the convent on the sly
So she can take her contraband
To sell in Hay-on-Wye.

For there she has a bookshop
Which is no more than a cover
For her calculated exploitation
Of the Reverend Mother.

Not satisfied with selling dope
And hooky hooch as well
She even runs a special sort of
Brothel from her cell,

For men who have a passion for
Perverted forms of fun,
Involving silent discipline
Inflicted by a nun.

She has bought a ranch in Canada
And a nightclub in Belize
With the profits she's been making
From her merry little wheeze.

And she's worked out that in two years' time,
She might reasonably aspire
To give the nuns their wimple back
And happily retire,

To Liechtenstein or Monaco
To live off the amount
Of cash accumulated in her offshore
Bank account.

She will be sorry when she leaves
And has to say goodbye.
Because she rather likes the nuns.
She hopes she doesn't cry.

The Risk of Rhayader

If you walk around Rhayader look at the ground
For all around Rhayader there can be found
A plant that's so rare that it's simply unique
To the Rhayader district – the man-eating leek.

There's unwary walkers on Pantllwyd Hill
Whose shades are out walking the mountainside still.
While their bones as they desiccate silently speak
Of the danger that's posed by the man-eating leek.

It grows between rocks about eight inches tall
But inside the leek tightly rolled in a ball
Is a twenty-foot stalk with a sort of harpoon
It can shoot out like lightning from April to June.

And the poisonous sap on the end of these stalks
Means an agonized death for someone who walks
Too close to the plant. So make sure that you seek
For the signs that you're close to the man-eating leek.

For once you've been stung you will have to endure
The vegetable toxin for which there's no cure
And it reels you back in once it feels you go still
To the heart of the plant to digest you at will.

There's no need to worry once midsummer's over.
Then the man-eating leek is as harmless as clover.
But when April comes round and it has to set seed
The man-eating leek's a most dangerous weed.

The January Sales in Newport

I saw her last night with a scowl on her face.
She looked at me once and said "you disgrace,
Just look at yourself in the mirror by there.
Just look at the state of your shoes, of your hair.
You've got a good figure. What is it you lack?
When were you dragged through a hedge on your back?
I tell you," she told me, "enough is enough.
I will not go out anymore with a scruff."

And that's why you find me this morning by here,
Dragged round the shops in the sales by the ear,
Kitted out smart in new trousers and shirt,
Bereft of all fag ash, and creases and dirt.
And proof of the dictum I've heard people say,
Give in with good grace, it's the easiest way.

The thing from Llyn Trawsfynydd

Through the frosted window pane while everybody sleeps
The thing from Llyn Trawsfynydd breathes upon the glass and peeps
At all the people slumbering inside their cozy beds
With nothing of them showing on their pillows but their heads.

The thing from Llyn Trawsfynydd doesn't see what you would see
If you were looking through the glass at folk like you and me.
The thing from Llyn Trawsfynydd contemplates a different view,
Regarding us as breakfast when he looks at me and you.

And the locals from Trawsfynydd if they've got an ounce of sense
Prefer an eight-foot solid wall to a flimsy wooden fence,
And checking doors and windows before they go to bed,
And getting home before it's dark, instead of being dead.

They never visit neighbours and don't stay out once it's dark
Or let their children out of sight when playing in the park.
And very seldom will the people from Trawsfynydd go
Within a gunshot of the lake, not knowing what they know.

But notwithstanding all their care, and all their cautious fears,
It's seldom that a month goes by that no one disappears.
And so the locals, being wise, endeavour to ensure
A visitor is still outside before they bolt the door.

Ffynnon Islwyn Morris

Islwyn Morris was fifty-seven and had been a librarian since he was nineteen. Strictly speaking he had only been a librarian since he was twenty-two following his graduation in the appropriate examinations after a period of study in college, but it was at the age of nineteen that his studies had commenced, and so it was from that age that he had set in his own mind the commencement date for his career as a librarian. For the more romantically minded of us we might set the commencement date as some fourteen years before that because, from the first day of his infant schooling when he had walked past the delights of the little collection of books that existed under the imposing title of the school library, Islwyn Morris had been hooked. He loved the look of books. He loved the smell and the touch and the sound of books. In his more intimate moments he even loved the taste of books. Hay-on-Wye was his 'promised land'; Blaenavon the new Jerusalem that had descended over The Gorenge to the Heads of the Valleys. Perhaps the only really significant aspect of books to which Islwyn Morris had not succumbed was their contents. Those books which dealt with how to become a librarian Islwyn Morris had delved into with assiduity but, otherwise, he considered it sacrilege to desecrate the page of a book by exposing it to the fading effects of wicked daylight. Dust was reprehensible. Oily finger printing hands, especially of the young, were anathema. To avoid any confusion, although I have alluded not only to Islwyn Morris' twenty-second and nineteenth years, and also to years earlier than those, Islwyn Morris was never guilty of the heinous crime of youth. The ten little tots who tottered into Miss Prothero's class in

Ysgol Llanbrynmair all those years and more ago included in their number one little old man. Not in appearance, as an inspection of the appropriate archived edition of the *Tal-y-bont and Pont Newydd Bugle* will show – should you wish to look – but in every other way Islwyn Morris was fifty-seven from the day he was five. He doddered and he fussed, he was thinning on top and thickening round the waist and became instantly set in his ways as soon as he was old enough to have any ways. And he always wore a cardigan and a knitted tie even when forced to play cricket. He only played cricket when he was forced and never played anything else ever, and it was not very long before nobody even bothered forcing him to play cricket and he was allowed to tend the school library whilst all his peers were fast becoming flannelled fools.

It is therefore sadly ironic that Islwyn Morris was made redundant from his post as head librarian on the day he reached his fifty-seventh birthday. Most people thought, and not a few hoped, that he would pine away and die once excised from the library service but, to universal surprise he took his redundancy money, sold his house in Upper Cwm-twrch and bought a derelict smallholding not far from Llangrannog. But it was not actually not far from Llangrannog; it was actually *very* far from Llangrannog but, for reasons that will become clear later, it is probably best that you do not know exactly where it was that Islwyn Morris bought his smallholding, and not far from Llangrannog will do for the good reason that if the smallholding had to be near somewhere, then being near Llangrannog would give you as good an idea where it was near without actually telling you the location. Please understand that I only record the place as being near Llangrannog because it has to be near somewhere.

The smallholding was a nice smallholding as smallholdings go, nestled in a little valley into which the sun shone once a year on midsummer's day unless it was raining (which it always was) and along which you had a nice view of Cardigan Bay. It was seldom possible to enjoy the distant view of the sea because the prevailing wind whipped down the valley with all the ferocity of an avenging angel in a bad mood and stung your eyes and forced you indoors three-hundred-and-forty days of the year. On the other twenty-five days the valley was six feet deep in snow and the mountains shrouded in fog. If you were lucky, in a leap year, you might get a glimpse of blue-grey, but you had to be quick. Somehow or other, whilst he was farming his books in the libraries of the Gwendraeth and Amman valleys, Islwyn Morris had found the time to learn to drive and he had bought himself a second-hand post office van that had been hand painted with a thick green paint that had not been entirely successful in obliterating the Royal Mail crest on the side and rear doors. The crests winked at one dimly through the intermittent overcoats in certain lights. Islwyn Morris' neighbours in the valley looked upon him with the same suspicion as they looked upon all outsiders and, when his accent was deduced, that he came from somewhere outlandish beyond the Teifi Valley and was therefore not to be trusted at any price – so they didn't. Once a week he went to Cardigan market. In Cardigan market he bought fresh fish under the stone columns and wept inwardly at the second hand books. In Cardigan market he spoke infrequently and also in Cardigan he went to church. Being a librarian he could hardly go to chapel. He knew in his reverential heart that God had called him to higher things that Wesleyan non-conformity. His sacred call as a librarian showed him the true light of his worth and in Cardigan he found Anglicanism high enough for even his high calling. There was the lovely 1662 *Prayer Book*, too good to read, and a Bible treated like all library books should have been treated and chained to a lectern so that nobody could take it away. Indeed, if only the other seven communicants had taken the same pains as he to have gotten the whole of the prayer book and psalms by heart, there would have been no need for the service books and Psalters to have left their beautiful arrangements on the shelves. As he sat and saw the sinful handling, and even more sinful reading of books that should have been properly stored and displayed, he pondered in his heart on the wickedness of all flesh and shuddered at the eternal end of the scattered flock amongst which he sat at matins and evensong. The hymn books he did not mind being handed out as hymn books hardly counted as books at all, although he did debate within himself if they might not count as manuscripts, but he would let the thought pass as it troubled his communion with his maker. He once –during a particularly long sermon, in excess of ten minutes – speculated upon the status of the rows of *Hymns Ancient and Modern*, which he knew to contain not only hymns but also orders of service. Theology though was never his strong point and he went back to dozing as more appropriate for a true Christian in church.

Islwyn Morris' high Anglicanism did not endear him to his new neighbours either and they had little to do with each other, although they would sometimes meet at the cattle sales in Llanybydder. As nothing grew in his valley except rancour, Islwyn Morris raised sheep or, rather, placed sheep out to die, as nothing much would live in the valley either, and slowly his small-holding, which had only appeared derelict when he had bought it, fell into deeper dereliction. It did not collapse all at once as had his career as a librarian but, by the spring after he had moved in, it was becoming clear that the collapse was going to be as complete as it was inevitable. Just after Easter he left the cold, damp, mouldering sitting room of the leaky cottage that he had thought would become a bibliophilic idyll, and clambered on to the edge of the old well in the garden that never once yielded the fresh, spring, valley water that was going to be processed in the bottling plant that was going o be built in the old barn, the new roof of which and the new quipment of which were going to be paid for by the profits of he first year's lamb harvest. He gazed down into the fathomless lepths of the well whence no water had ever come, and prepared imself for the drop.

"Oh what will tomorrow bring?" he asked into the blackness is he flexed at the knees.

"Tomorrow it will be overcast with drizzle in the morning. In he afternoon there will be heavier rain from the west," said a voice rom down the well. "Laughing Boy will win the three-thirty at Kempton Park, Mrs Parry from Tyngoch will have twins although he doctors have told her there is only one girl and Mr Parry is he father of neither."

"Pardon?" said Islwyn Morris, rather taken aback and forgetting suicide for a moment in his curiosity at the strangeness of the voice. He looked around to see whence it had come.

"I said," said the voice, and there was no mistaking that it came from down the well: "Tomorrow it will be overcast with drizzle in he morning. In the afternoon there will be heavier rain from the west. Laughing Boy will win the three-thirty at Kempton Park, Mrs Parry from Tyngoch will have twins although the doctors have told her there is only one girl and Mr Parry is the father of neither."

"Who says so?" demanded Islwyn Morris.

"I do," said the voice.

"And how do you know?"

"I'm an oracle."

"You're a what?"

"An oracle. You know what an oracle is, you being a librarian." The voice was female and getting rather strident.

"Well of course I know what an oracle is," said Islwyn Morris, getting rather strident himself. "And I also know that oracles don't exist. I rather suspect that you are one of the girls from the village trying to make a fool out of me."

"Well I wouldn't have to try very hard would I," riposted the oracle, actually sounding rather like one of the girls from the village in its petulance. "Now if you don't mind, I'd rather you didn't jump down here, I've already got a couple of crows that have fallen in and a litter of puppies that the owners before last threw down. It takes years to get the smell out."

Islwyn Morris clambered down from the wall and leaned over.

"Where are you hiding?" he said.

"I'm not hiding anywhere I'm down here. I've told you, I'm an oracle."

"What do oracles look like?"

"They look like me of course. Dopey."

"Well I can't see you, it's too dark."

"Well I can see you. I can see right up your nose," said the oracle, tittering.

Islwyn Morris jumped back, embarrassed.

"I still think you're one of the village girls having fun. What did you say would win the three-thirty at Kempton Park?"

"Laughing Boy. Fourteen to one s.p."

"What's going to win the two o'clock at Chepstow?" asked Islwyn Morris suspicious still, but thinking at least he could go and check that on the television in ten minutes' time.

"There is no two o'clock at Chepstow. There are no races at Chepstow until next Saturday when the races will be won in the following sequence: Ariadne, Garners' Delight, The Sea Conquest, Scoot For Trouble, Wapitii and Goldust of the East. If you place a one pound accumulator on that lot you would win seven hundred and fifty six thousand, two hundred and seven pounds fourteen shillings and sixpence provided you pay tax on the bet. I'm sorry disregard the odd fourteen and six, I keep forgetting the money's changed."

"I don't believe you," said Islwyn Morris, not believing the voice.

"Suit yourself," said the voice. "Your loss not mine."

"How do I know you're telling the truth?"

"I'm a bloody oracle. Of course I'm telling the truth. What sort of oracle would I be if I didn't tell the truth? There's no point in being a bloody oracle if you don't tell the truth is there? I might as well be one of the girls out of the village if all I was going to do was sit down a well and spout a load of nonsense."

"The oracle at Delphi didn't always tell the truth," reasoned Islwyn Morris, not unreasonably.

"Yes she did. Honest as the day was long. She just used to be ambiguous that's all. That was her style. We all have our own way of doing things."

"Alright then," said Islwyn Morris. "Predict me something else that I can prove and I'll believe you."

"Throw me down some money first. You've had a freebie; you're not getting any more."

Islwyn Morris threw down a ten pence piece. He did not hear it hit bottom.

"Ten pence," said the voice, full of derision. "You cheapskate. I'm not predicting for ten pence. What sort of oracle do you think I am?"

"One that lives in the village and wears hooped ear-rings and a denim skirt two sizes too small for her with a tattoo of a butterfly in the small of her back. That sort of oracle."

"Silly bugger. I am an ephemeral being without substance, I have no ears in which to wear ear-rings nor epidermis upon which to etch a tattoo. Mind you if I had legs – which I don't – I bet they'd be nice legs and look good in a micro-mini. I can manifest myself under certain circumstances. I might have a go at that, a nice pair of pins and a tiny, short skirt. Not for a silly old, baldy-headed bugger like you though. I shall wait until that nice Simon Jones, the cricketer, comes to the village on holiday next October. He's hunky, drop-dead gorgeous."

"What about my prediction?"

"I've told you, not for ten pence."

"How much?"

"Two hundred quid."

"I do not possess two hundred pounds in the entire world. If I had pounds I would not be throwing myself down wells, infested with oracles or otherwise."

"You have a pound in your pocket. I know you have, you found it by the stile yesterday where that hiker dropped it and you didn't call after him to tell him so, you just trousered it and went away. Do you know if you had called him back he'd have missed his bus at the cross roads and have had to wait for the next one two hours later."

"Well I did him a favour then, didn't I," stated Islwyn Morris.

"Not really," replied the oracle. "If he had been on the later bus he wouldn't have been in time to turn left instead of right when he got off at Llanelli outside the Tinopolis studios and get run down and killed by a brewer's dray."

"I don't believe you," said Islwyn Morris, not believing the voice again.

"Go in and put on the wireless, it's just about to come on the Radio Cymru news. Third item after the bit about the price the supermarkets pay farmers for their milk going down again."

Not believing the voice Islwyn Morris went into the kitchen and turned on the wireless set. Sure enough the third item on the news was about a stranger being run over and killed and police wanting any information. The description fitted that of the legitimate owner of Islwyn Morris' last pound coin. He went back out to the well.

"Oi," he shouted down the well. "Are you still there?"

"I'm an oracular well," answered the oracle, disgruntled in the extreme to be oied at. "I'm hardly likely to be anywhere else than down a well am I. Pillock."

"No need to be rude. I believe you. I want a prediction."

"Say please."

"Alright then. Please."

"Two hundred pounds."

"I've only got a pound, I told you."

"I don't need you to tell me," riposted the oracle, really getting rather annoyed. "I'm a bloody oracle. I know precisely what you've got in your pocket. I also know you've got fifty quid in the Post Office that you've forgotten about."

"I'd forgotten about that," said Islwyn Morris, remembering.

"Bloody hell," said the oracle, who stamped the foot it had been manifesting for practice for when Simon Jones the hunky Glamorgan cricketer came next October.

"You are rather foul mouthed," observed Islwyn Morris, who was now convinced that the voice was after all, as it claimed, an oracle and was rather surprised to hear it use bad language. "Do all oracles swear?"

"You'd make a bloody parson swear Islwyn Morris. You really would," said the oracle, losing its temper.

"Well if it makes you feel better I believe you are an oracle. May I have my prediction now please?"

"Two hundred pounds."

"I've only got a pound."

"Well take it down to the village and put it on Way to Romp in the next race at York. Then put the whole lot on Sally's Sweetheart at Uttoxeter and you'll have over five hundred pounds. Come back here and I'll give you a prediction."

Islwyn Morris went into the village, not for the first time, and into the bookmakers which *was* for the first time and put a one pound bet on Way to Romp at York. He did not get back quite as much as he thought he would because he had not prepaid the tax but being a librarian he soon got the hang of it and came back with over four hundred pounds.

"Cooee," he yelled down the well. "Come and get it. And he threw two fat bundles of notes into the blackness. There was a silence for a few seconds before the voice of the oracle bellowed up.

"Not in notes you drongo. What's the good of paper money down here? It's going all soggy and limp. I need gold and silver and precious metals. Oh you are a toe-rag."

"You never said."

"I shouldn't need to say. It's just plain common sense."

"What about my prediction?"

"You're not getting one."

"I've paid. I want my prediction."

"The ratings for *Coronation Street* will go down before Christmas."

"That's not a prediction."

"Yes it is."

"Well it's no use to me. I don't watch soap operas."

"Yes you do, you watch *Pobl y Cwm*."

"That's not a soap opera. I want a proper prediction that will do me some good. Go on and I'll make sure that the next lot is in gold."

"Oh alright then. Red Rag at Catford dogs tonight."

Red Rag romped home and Islwyn Morris threw a tip down the well in the shape of a diamond ring. The oracle was pleased with that and gave him a five hundred to one outsider at Longchamps. That got it a double row choker and some pearl drops. A Yankee at Devon and Exeter bought a new roof for the cottage, a new Land Rover Discovery and a very thick silver bangle that the oracle thought might catch the eye of Simon Jones, the hunky Glamorgan cricketer when he came there next October.

"You are getting too fat," the oracle told him. "You must lose weight."

"I'll be alright," said Islwyn Morris. "A bit of weight is good for me."

"You'll be sorry," said the oracle.

"Yeah, whatever," replied Islwyn Morris, eating an éclair. He had never been able to afford éclairs by the dozen when he was a librarian. At the time he had thought it a price worth paying but was beginning to have his doubts now that éclairs were so easy to come by.

By July the smallholding had been landscaped and the barn converted into an eight-bedroom luxury library. Islwyn Morris had put on three stones and was getting all of his clothes hand-made. He was finding it harder to place bets but, by using a series of go betweens, he was still making a living slightly in excess of two million pounds a week. The well seemed to have an infinite capacity for jewellery, and he had even, at the oracle's request, thrown down a near complete set of *Wisden* so that it could bone up on Glamorgan cricket before October.

By late September Islwyn Morris had put of eight stones in weight and waddled to the well to get his bets. It was a beautiful late evening for once. Islwyn Morris was dressed only in shorts and flip-flops. He knew the weather would be fine, the oracle had told him so.

"Hallo," he called down the well. "How are we old oracular font of all knowledge?"

"Go away," said the oracle.

"Don't be an old misseryguts," said Islwyn Morris, sucking the cream out of an éclair.

"Go away. I don't want to talk to you."

"Why not? I thought we were pals. I've invited Simon Jones, that hunky cricketer from Glamorgan to stay chez Morris, all expenses paid and a nice fat retainer for doing a day's coaching at the local school. He's agreed to come. I did that all for you. I'll tell you what, if that was you I saw flitting about the yard last night and walking through the cowshed wall in that micro-mini, those legs look pretty top of the bill to me."

"Go away, he's not coming and it's your entire fault."

"What do you mean he's not coming? I've just been on the phone to his agent, the deal's all signed."

"He's not coming and it's your entire fault."

"How's it all my fault?"

"Because you wouldn't listen to my predictions."

"Of course I listen to your predictions. I've put money on every one. I'm a multi-millionaire. I'd be some sort of wally not to listen to your predictions. What are you on about?" He sucked the last of the cream from the éclair and tossed the case into the grass where a magpie came and flew off with it. Magpies had got into the habit of following Islwyn Morris around for discarded éclair cases.

"No you don't listen to my predictions."

"Yes I do."

"No you don't."

"What predictions don't I listen to?"

"Don't go putting on too much weight or you'll be sorry. And now because of that Simon Jones the hunky Glamorgan cricketer won't be coming. Oh I hate you."

"Why won't he be coming?"

"Because you are going to mysteriously disappear and so there will be no one to pay him and he's not coming and it's your entire selfish fault after I've manifested this lovely body and the best pair of legs you or Simon Jones the hunky Glamorgan cricketer or anyone else has ever seen. And I've even got a tattoo of a butterfly in the small of my back. It'll take me ages to demanifest all this lot and instead of the most gorgeous Welshman for centuries I'm going to be stuck with you, all because you couldn't leave off the bloody éclairs. Oh I hate you."

"How on earth are a few cakes going to do all that?" asked Islwyn Morris, not believing the oracle for once.

"Because a bloody great bull is going to come through that gate and you are going to try to run away to the house which six months ago you could have done easily, but now you're so fat you can't run anywhere and the bull is going to toss you and gore you and throw you down this well which is bottomless, so no-one is ever going to find your corpse and I'm going to have you down here all disembowelled and rotting and decomposing and stinking the well out for decades instead of sleeping with Simon Jones the hunky cricketer from Glamorgan. Oh it's so unfair."

"Oh don't be silly," said Islwyn Morris, reassuring her. "Look. If it makes you feel better I promise I'll go on a strict diet. Look, just to set your mind at rest I'll go and lock the gate to the lane."

He turned to waddle down to the gate but his path was barred by a huge Welsh Black bull, pawing the ground and snorting at him. He turned to run and a voice drifted up from the well.

"Oh, it's so bloody unfair."

Mefin Caradoc Bevan

Mefin Caradoc Bevan was a man of forty-four years. He had a waistcoat, a bowler hat, a watch on a chain across his broad expanse of stomach engraved with the initials G.W.R., a superfluity of chins and a mother. There was a time, in his extreme youth, when Mefin Caradoc Bevan had a father too, an engine driver working out of Carmarthen sheds but, on a day trip to Aberaeron, utilizing one of the free tickets to which the family were entitled, his mother, who was young then, had found his father talking to a loose young woman from Llansanffraid. It shows you how long ago this all was because it was in the days when there was still a railway line to Aberaeron and when you could still go by train to Newcastle Emlyn, albeit that was the end of the world according to Mefin's mother.

The young woman to whom his father was talking to had not only painted her fingernails, she had also painted her toenails and put henna in her hair. His mother who, even then had more of the starch about her than was necessarily good for her, had watched how her husband, and this latter-day Jezebel spoke. The conversation lasted for a good twenty or thirty seconds and ended with the brazen harlot leaping up onto the tip of her painted toes and planting a kiss on her husband's cheek. For as long as he bothered to protest, Mefin's father suggested that the woman had been a complete stranger and had asked the way to Alban Square but, as Mefin's mother quite reasonably reasoned, why would a woman, with or without painted toenails who came from Llansanffraid, want to know the way to Alban Square. The fact that she didn't, and was only finding an excuse to plant a kiss on the cheek of the handsome young engine driver with the happy smile whom she often saw when she caught the train from Aberaeron into Lampeter, was neither here nor there. Mefin's mother knew by heart exactly what it said in the fourteenth verse of the twentieth chapter of the Book of Exodus. "Na odineba!"

In truth, although she was a married woman, she was not exactly sure of the upper and lower limits prescribed by that particular commandment, but she was certain that allowing oneself to be kissed by a woman from Llansanffraid with painted toenails must constitute a breach of the law, if not in total then in detail. From that day forth she saw her husband in a new light and she commenced a detailed vivisection of his soul that ended in him turning to drink and eventually hanging himself from the gantry of the outer home signal at Briton Ferry Junction Signal Box two years later while he was waiting at the signal for the road on the ten fifteen down coal train from Onllwyn Washery. Mefin's mother went into deep mourning for the rest of her life and determined that Mefin would grow up impermeable to the effects of drink and women with painted toenails.

That is where we came in. Mefin had followed his father into the railway (they were family concerns in those days), and had risen through the ranks: from porter, to leading porter, to signalman, to signalman's inspector and, at the age of forty-four, he was a relief station master with a waist that was twice his inside leg, and a deacon in Bethania Chapel. In his buttonhole he would wear a red rosebud, and one day, when the line superintendent deemed him to be old enough, and wise enough, he would be a permanent station master, first at one of the smaller stations, later at Carmarthen, or perhaps Llanelli. There were those who knew about these things who said that there was nothing to stop him from one day rising to the great height of station master in Swansea itself. Mefin did not consider these things, although his mother heard them from time to time and treasured them up in her heart and considered them in the long winter evenings when he was on late turn a long way from home station. The two of them lived quietly together in the neat, trim, tidy house in Pencader with its neat, trim, tidy garden and vegetables in the back and a canary in the window, and talked of nothing much other than his mother's health and the wickedness of the world and of all women – except his mother!

Until he had run to fat, or rather been force-fed by his mother, Mefin had inherited some of his father's rugged good looks and once or twice the maidens of the parish set a cap at him. They were no match for Mefin's mother and she saw them off with little trouble and he was not long into his twenties when all thoughts of women passed from him and he passed from the thoughts of all women. He had a morbid fear of drink and he found the most onerous of his duties to be going into the station hotels to check on the books or inspecting the station buffets. He also had a morbid fear of his mother and, to him, she was the great central theme of all life. He knew nothing and saw nothing, save those things that his mother bade him know or showed him. His was a well-ordered life in which his mother did the ordering and he drew the benefits that she advised him of.

Strange to tell then, although he should have been alien to all around him, he was in fact liked and admired in almost equal proportions by everyone with whom he came in contact. By the railwaymen he was admired because he knew his business and knew it well. By the congregation of the chapel he was admired for his selfless attention to the duties of a deacon and by his unswerving moral rectitude and an honest and caring heart. Mefin was kind and he was kindly. He would have been generous but he gave his wages each week to his mother and she gave him his board and keep in return and bought his underwear at the rate of one pair of combinations each year and, therefore, Mefin had nothing with which to be generous.

Except of course – time. He had a little of that on his hands between going to work and coming back from work. At all other times he was the property of his mother and followed her about rather in the fashion of a staid collie dog. He carried her bags and he waited for her. He sat with her at spinster teas and ate buttered toast when it was given to him and minded his manners in silence until it was time to go home. His outer garments consisted of a winged collar and dick bow on a Sunday, bought from Manchester House in Pencader, which is no longer there, and the rest of the week was his old working clothes patched and ironed, darned and revived until the next suit was issued.

There was only one issue with which his mother did not hold instant and absolute sway, and that was in the matter of smiling. Mefin would insist on smiling. He had a soft, kindly smile that bespoke a warm heart and a selfless nature and for all his mother's cold, calculated veneering of the boy into manhood, the smile would surface and people would like Mefin will she or nil she; and nil she did to her utmost. Mefin's smile, which was something he had inherited from his father, was a constant burning knife in the very heart of his mother and she wept sometimes in vexation that through four decades she had not been able to eliminate it from her son. She prayed most earnestly every morning and every evening that before she died she would see and know for a certainty that her son would never smile again. Only then would she feel confident that he would be safe from all the fleshly wickedness of the world and women with henna in their hair and paint on their nails.

It came one day before Mefin's mother had cured him of smiling completely, that he was called to the line superintendent's office and told that he was going to be promoted to the post of station master at Llanbedr-Pont-Steffan, or Lampeter to you and me. This news was as unusual as it was unexpected and came from a concatenation of events that might have been thought of as due to some supernatural influence, which for those of you who finish this story I leave to you to decide if it was or if it was not.

Not only were there three men senior to Mefin who should have had the post before him, but there was also an incumbent with still five more years to go until he retired from the railway service. However the incumbent had been struck by a runaway trolley of milk churns and had been precipitated under the seven twenty-one stopping train to Aberystwyth. He was carried to the hospital on a shutter with his left leg in a wheelbarrow alongside and died the next day from loss of blood and a significant breach of the rules and regulations. The next in line had suddenly found that he had been left as the sole heir to a minor baronetcy in Liverpool and had gone away to be knighted and take up an altogether different station in life. The second in line had been found administering sedative soaked corn to the racing pigeons and laying bets on the eventual outcomes of the races in the certain knowledge that all those to which he had been slipping mickey finns would never get further than the station yard where he kept a cat on short commons who ensured that the chances of any birds finding their way back to the loft was on the slim side. The third candidate married the widowed landlady of a hotel in Rhyl and decided that he would throw himself into the family business at the expense of his railway career. So, most suddenly, the paths to preferment unexpectedly became clear for Mefin and he came home that night and broke the news to his mother. They would have to leave Pencader, of course, and move to Lampeter, but there was a good strict chapel there and, although there was a university college, it was a theological one, albeit Church in Wales. The station master's house in Lampeter had another advantage; it was close to the station. The advantage of that was that the station was on the other side of the river to the town and thus could only be approached by way either of the main road bridge or, alternatively, by the small footbridge just a little upstream of the station. Furthermore the station master's house stood in its own grounds and thus even from the station itself there was a clear field of view from the house whereby anyone with painted toenails would have been clearly visible to Mefin's mother long before they could have reached the door with their blandishments and winning ways.

The station at Lampeter did have one disadvantage and that was to be found in the ticket office in the shape of Miss Gwenllian Pugh, a spinster of thirty-seven summers. True she had a nose that almost met her chin and eyes that would have done sterling service on a myopic pig and her hair had a tendency to extreme wispiness, and she was devoid of any shape whatsoever. But she did have fingernails, and Mefin's mother followed an inevitable chain of logic that lead her to deduce that in that case she would in all probability have toenails and that both fingernails and toenails were perfectly capable of being painted. Miss Gwenllian Pugh lived with her widowed mother and three cats in a small cottage just by the main road near the river bridge, not far from where the Co-op now stands. For this reason Mefin's mother insisted that Mefin always journey to and from the town by way of the northern bridge to ensure that he avoided at all costs the possibility of his falling under the spell of Miss Gwenllian Pugh, bereft of her blue serge uniform jacket and skirt and painted to the eyeballs. This scheme, sound as it may have seemed to Mefin's mother, and to you without the benefit of hindsight, only went to prove the truth of the adage paraphrased by the Scottish poet Mr Rabbie Burns that the best laid schemes of mice and men "gang aft agley". I am sure that such a wise and astute person as a poet would not have missed the point that not only the best laid schemes of mice and men might unexpectedly "gang aft agley", but that the best laid schemes of women too had as much propensity for "agleyness" as any laid by the average man or mouse. Indeed, this particular scheme of the determined relict of the late locomotive driver Bevan agleyed most spectacularly and in a most unexpected way. It occurred in the following manner.

Mefin, and Mefin's mother, had been ensconced in regal estate in the station master's house for some six months. We know it was six months because the time coincided exactly with the changes from the autumn to the spring timetables. During those cold winter months Mefin had been practically confined to barracks to keep him out of the clutches of the hordes of sirens who occupied the Gomorrah of Lampeter, with its university college and shops selling items of female attire, the function of which Mefin could only guess. The only time he was allowed out, other than to go to work, where Mefin's mother knew he would be proof against all attacks by his strict regard for the protocols and distinctions that separate so grand a functionary as a station master from the more lowly parts of creation (the highest of which was the chief clerk), were three times each Sunday to chapel, where again Mefin was proof from any chance of slip or fall by the fact that Mefin's mother ensured that, not only did she accompany him at all times to a distance of no more than fifteen feet, but also that he was supplied with his own and a spare hymn book to obviate even the remotest possibility of his having to share.

Mefin's mother used those intervening six winter months to provide herself with such a fierce reputation around the town that, by the spring, she felt secure enough in her position and her plans that when she succumbed (doctors said due to the proximity of the dampness of the water meadows of the River Teifi) to an acute case of bronchitis, Mefin was allowed to walk into Lampeter town to purchase for her a quarter of mentholated lozenges. Mefin's mother's doctor had assured her that she would find immediate and lasting relief from the agonies of bronchitis only through the medium of either Evans' Oil rubbed upon her chest or mentholated lozenges. The prospect of rubbing Evans' Oil on even her own chest smacked to Mefin's mother of a carnality only to be found in the temples of Dagon in the Book of Samuel and, therefore, she decided upon what seemed to her to be a course of action that held no chance of temptation. It only goes to show how wrong one can be. Well is the Evil One described as a roaring lion going about seeking whom he may devour? In fairness to her, Mefin's mother was not a woman to let down her guard and it may be that in her solicitous concern for the purity of her son and her insistence that all of Mefin's trips were made by way of the upstream bridge to ensure he arrived into town, giving the home of the temptress Miss Gwenllian Pugh the widest of possible berths, she overlooked the security of her own soul. Mefin's mother was an abstemious woman but, like most people who take stringent steps to avoid falling into vice, when they do succumb to temptation they tend to succumb in a grand manner. Rather like the man who couldn't stop hanging his whippets – but that is another story that does not need to concern us here. A diet, whose most extreme indulgence was a single cup of black, sugarless, herbal tea taken with great ceremony before retiring to bed on a Friday night, was no guard against the lascivious and vaporous temptations of the flesh posed by menthol once they were unsuspectedly indulged in. Those mentholated lozenges were to Mefin's mother as Uriah's wife to King David. Once they first entered between her lips she was like the Lotus eaters of whom the poet Homer informs us. Mefin's mother indulged herself in the intoxicating perfume which ascended like the savours of a pagan sacrifice, and the entire quarter was gone before the going down of the sun the following day. Mefin's mother attempted to resist the urge for indulgence but her defences were all on the outside, rather like the Maginot Line, they were easily bypassed. It is a shame, and as things turned out indeed an irony that the French Ministère de la Defénse did not make a case study of Mefin's mother – they may have learnt something to have saved their land from the occupying tyranny of the jackboot some several years later.

Mefin's mother spent a night of agony in a restless craving for mentholated lozenges. All through the night little dragons kept popping out of her wardrobe with her corsets on their heads and whispered into her ear as she struggled to sleep the delights of mentholated lozenges. As she reached for her glass of water from the dresser in the morning, her hand shook and she was reduced to sniffing the empty bag in which the mentholated lozenges had arrived. There were a few shards of lozenge and some sugar grains lingering in the furthest recesses of the bag and she greedily tore the paper back and licked at them like one of those Foreign Legionnaires one hears about crawling over the burning sands of the Sahara Desert with their tongues and lips all swollen and blistered and coming, quite unexpectedly and just in the nick of time, upon an oasis.

Mefin's mother went down to her breakfast of thin porridge gruel and whey milk but found no solace in feasting. She was in need of a mentholated lozenge. The craving was desperate and nothing, not even a cup of her herbal tea, even though it was not Friday, could satisfy the wanting and the longing. Without washing up she donned her shawl and set out for the town. She hurried along the road and over the river bridge, not even pausing to glare at the siren Miss Gwenllian Pugh's den of a cottage. Mefin's mother had one fixed and all consuming thought. She must have a mentholated lozenge. Had someone passed that instant sucking a mentholated lozenge, she had already worked out that she would attack them with her umbrella and force them to spit it out. There were no degradations to which she would not stoop. Why she would even have been civil to Miss Gwenllian Pugh's mother if that widowed dam of a dissolute vixen had at that moment appeared with a packed of mentholated lozenges.

No such extremity occurred and Mefin's mother entered Cardigan House and bought, for the princely sum of three farthings, one half pound of mentholated lozenges. Mefin's mother had sufficient shreds of her old dignity not to tear into the bag in the open street. Somehow knowing that the mentholated lozenges were there helped a little with the cravings and she managed to return to the station master's house before consuming the first one, although she did have several furtive sniffs of the bag along the way. By three o'clock in the afternoon Mefin's mother had eaten the whole bag and was starting to get delirium tremens. There was nothing for it but to go back into Lampeter and buy some more mentholated lozenges. They would look askance in Cardigan House but Mefin's mother had already worked out a plan. She would tell Mrs Edwards, the owner of the shop, that they were not for her but for another and that the other had mislaid the bag of mentholated lozenges and being too unwell herself to walk all the way back into town she had asked her, Mefin's mother, if she would go and replace the lost lozenges. She even thought of getting the next train down to Tregaron and buying her mentholated lozenges there where she was not known.

Whilst she was communing thus with her indomitable soul, Mefin came in. She had forgotten that it was his half-day and that he would be coming home early. Mefin was taken aback that the cleaning had not been done and that there were still the dirty plates from breakfast in the sink and he considered that perhaps his mother was more ill than he had thought. He asked her if he should call the doctor once more, but Mefin's mother insisted that all would be well. She informed him that she had been having a little trouble with her breathing and had therefore gone for a gentle stroll down by the river. Then a brainwave hit Mefin's mother in the manner one will often do to those who are desperate. She told Mefin that she had succumbed to a fit of coughing brought upon by the cold spring air and had dropped her bag of mentholated lozenges in the water. She asked Mefin to go back into Lampeter and buy her another quarter of mentholated lozenges. The thought that there would be lozenges again before the evening eased her cravings a little and she gave Mefin a list of other things that she wanted. Before she had finished the list she had changed the quarter of a pound to a half a pound, and after she had finished the list but before she handed it to Mefin she had altered the half pound to a whole pound, "to save having to go out again before the weekend," as she explained to Mefin.

Mefin's mother had already determined that in the morning she would go to Carmarthen on the train where there were several pharmacists where she could buy several quarter pound bags of mentholated lozenges without arousing undue suspicion. Why, then she could go to Aberaeron, and Aberystwyth and all sorts of places. There was no reason for anyone in Lampeter to suspect that she was addicted to mentholated lozenges. Indeed, as she told herself, she was not addicted to mentholated lozenges; she could give them up at any time. Anyway, she had looked all through the Book of Leviticus and there was not a word about mentholated lozenges in there. Why should she not have the occasional mentholated lozenge if she felt like it, purely for medicinal purposes? In that manner did she commune with herself whilst Mefin was out getting her mentholated lozenges?

It was nearly six o'clock when Mefin returned from Lampeter with a bag full of things and a faint smell of menthol about him. The sun was starting to go down over the hills either side of the Aeron valley as he walked over the little bridge that spanned the

Teifi. Thinking of nothing in particular, Mefin was surprised to hear a voice singing. The voice was singing a song that went as follows, "Maladie d'amour, maladie de les jeunesse." It was a jolly little song but, as it was, as you have quite rightly observed, sung in French, Mefin was completely unable to understand it. Mefin had never met anyone on the bridge before and he said "hallo" to the air because he could not see whence came the song. It occurred to him that the song appeared to be coming from over the side of the bridge but that was ridiculous because there was nothing over the side of the bridge but the River Teifi, and no one would be singing songs in the River Teifi in a language that Mefin could not understand. They would be shouting "help" in a language that he did understand.

"Bonjour," came back the voice, light and lilting. The voice had a French accent.

"Pardon," said Mefin.

"Bonjour," said the voice again, and it sounded to Mefin even more as if it were coming from over the side of the bridge. Mefin's curiosity and credulity got the better of him and he went to the bridge parapet and looked over the downstream side.

"Bonjour," said the voice again in the friendliest manner and Mefin could quite plainly see that the voice came from a woman in the river. The woman had long dark-brown hair that hung over her shoulders and covered her chest. It was just as well that it did cover her chest because she had nothing else to cover her chest. She had a round plump face with the palest but brightest blue eyes that Mefin, or indeed anyone else, had ever seen and a rather Roman nose. She had the prettiest, prettiest smile and as she smiled up at Mefin she said "bonjour" again. In tossing her hair slightly to smile up at Mefin, the long tresses slipped back from her snowy white breasts and they bobbed slightly on the surface of the water. Mefin had never seen a naked woman's torso before, but he had to admit to himself that the plump, round full view before him, topped by white, smooth shoulders and that oh so pretty, pretty face with the smile and the bright blue eyes were not the dreadful spectre Mefin's mother had led him to believe. Mefin was really quite pleased too to find that he was not transmogrified into stone.

"Hallo," he said. "Who are you? What are you doing in the river?"

The vision of loveliness in the river smiled up at him once more and waved a perfectly formed, slightly plump but exquisitely shaped right arm at him, causing her breasts to rise and fall in a way that Mefin found most captivating. She spoke in a heavy French accent. Mefin did not know it was French. "I am a mermaid," said the mermaid.

"Are you really?" said Mefin. "What – sort of half woman and half fish? Do you have a fish's tail?"

The mermaid executed a back flip and her splendid, plump breasts and long dark hair and the oh-so-pretty smile and beautiful blue eyes disappeared under the rippling waters of the Teifi to be replaced by a long, elegant but indisputably piscine tail. It was a lovely shade of emerald green and covered in tight little scales. The tail waved twice, it might have been three times but Mefin did not notice (and it does not matter), and then flipped down into the water to be replaced by the plump breasts, the long hair, the oh-so-lovely smile and the brightest blue eyes you or anyone else had ever see.

"Oui," said the mermaid. "Do you not sink eet ees ze lovliest tail in ze 'ole wide world."

"It is rather splendid," affirmed Mefin. "Would you like a mentholated lozenge?"

"No sank you," answered the mermaid. "I would not mind a nice sardine eef you 'as one."

"I'm afraid not," said Mefin. "I'm very sorry."

"Eet iz no matter," said the mermaid, "I 'ave ze longing for sardines. I 'ave not 'ad a sardine for so many ages I cannot recall. Zere iz nossing but stickley-backs and ze tidlers in zis rivier. Ze trouts and se zalmonds I cannot catch because ze dratted water 'e iz too shallow to get a good dive at zem. Alors. I should not mind a leetle Cammembert Cheeze if you 'ave some."

"Sorry, I've only got Caerphilly."

"Desolé," said the mermaid with a sigh of disappointment. "You are very 'ansome. I will sing to you again." And the mermaid sang her jolly little song about young love once more. When she had finished she slipped below the surface and was gone. Mefin returned home to his mother but was wise enough not to say anything to her about the mermaid.

The next evening Mefin told his mother he was thinking of going for a little walk. He was expecting his mother to forbid it but he was going to tell her that he suspected that the lamp man was purloining the paraffin from the signal lamps and he wanted to catch him in the act. That he thought would be a reasonable excuse. Mefin was surprised to find that his mother, who was sucking a mentholated lozenge, seemed to be almost oblivious to his proposal. She waved a supine sort of hand at him and said "whatever" and went back to smiling beatifically out of the window at nothing that Mefin could discern. He thought that perhaps he would speak to the doctor again.

Mefin went direct to the bridge and looked over. The River Teifi ran swiftly through the arches and down the stony glides and he could see down into the shallows.

"Hallo," he called. "Are you there?"

There was no reply and he scanned the water anxiously for an oh-so-pretty smile and the bluest eyes he or you or I have ever seen. He watched the water for twenty minutes and was just about to leave when a great plume of icy cold river water hit him on the back of the neck and his bowler hat fell into the river. Mefin was astonished and soaked but delighted to see a beautiful round face with long brown hair appear twenty feet downstream with his bowler hat on its head. With two powerful flips of her tail the mermaid swam up underneath where Mefin was looking down.

"Bonjour," she said and waved an exquisite arm up at him.

Mefin had not wasted his time at work that day. He had been looking in the international codebook for overseas parcels and had discovered what "bonjour" meant.

"Bonjour," he replied, "comment allez-vous?"

"You must say tu to me," replied the mermaid. "I sink you eez very 'ansome and I am your friend. So you must say tu."

"How nice," said Mefin. "We do the same in Welsh, only we say chi and ti."

"Are you not an Eengleeshman?" asked the mermaid, looking puzzled.

"Most certainly not. I am Welsh."

"But you speak in Eengleesh."

"Yes, mother says a station master should speak in English as Welsh is for common persons."

"Zat ees why you are zo 'ansome," said the mermaid, obviously satisfied with the explanation to what was something of a conundrum to her. "Eet eez because you are not Eengleesh. I do not like ze Eengleesh. Zey coom and sinks all our sheeps, and ze poor mariners zey all drowns in ze sea because of ze Eengleesh. And zey 'ave made a mess of Dover 'arbour which was one of my favourite places when I was a leetle girl. I should 'ave sought zat ze Duke Villiaume he would 'ave changed zem by now but not so. Zis iz not Eenglend then?"

"Oh no, this is Wales," said Mefin.

"Sacre bleu," said the mermaid. "I must 'ave taken ze wrong

turning at Cap Finisterre. I thought ze water was a bit cold. Zat is what comes of asking directions from dolphins. Zey are most mischevious fishes. Mon papa told me always to beware of ze dolphins. Ah well it is no matter."

"I've brought you some sardines," ventured Mefin.

"Oh you are zo 'ansome and so kind."

"They're in a tin I'm afraid," said Mefin rather apologetically. "Shall I throw them down?"

"You weel 'ave to tak zem out of ze teen first," said the mermaid. "Ah do not 'ave ay 'ambag to keep ze teen openers een. Eef yo srow zem down one at a time I weel cetch zem."

Mefin did as he was bidden and, taking the key, peeled back the lid of the sardine tin. He took out the first sardine and dropped it gently into the upturned hands of the mermaid, trying not to look too long at her glorious, round, plump breasts floating on the shimmering surface of the River Teifi.

"Eek," screamed the mermaid as she caught the first sardine in her lovely, delicate, white hand, "eet iz covered in tomato sause. 'Ow disgusting. I weel 'ave to wash eet before I can eat it." Much to Mefin's disappointment she disappeared below the surface, but almost instantly came up again chewing. "You are so romanteek. You 'ave cuttid off ze 'eads of ze sardine. Yes I accept."

"I do not understand," said Mefin, not understanding. "You accept what."

"Your proposal of marriage. You are so very 'ansome and so very romantic. I weel marry you. I would not marry you eef you was Eengleesh because ze Eenglish they are so perfide but you are Gallois and zat is alright."

"I do not understand," said Mefin, still not understanding.

"You 'ave cut off ze 'ead of ze sardine. If a mer-homme he cut off ze 'ead of ze sardine before 'ee give 'im to ze mermaid zen 'ee is saying Will you marry me? You Welsmen you are so romantic. But first you must ask your papa 'eef you can marry. It would not be right otherwise."

"I'm afraid I don't have a papa, only a mama," answered Mefin, who now understood perfectly.

"Zat, is all one," said the mermaid, swallowing another sardine. "You can ask your mama."

"I don't think my mama will like the idea, she's not very keen on girls."

"I am not a girl, I am a mermaid," protested the mermaid with an air of Gallic petulance.

"I don't think she will say yes all the same," said Mefin, starting to feel a little disappointed.

"Zen I shall put a curse on her and turn her into an ugly old harridan," threatened the mermaid, who sank below the surface for a moment to ask a passing crayfish to fetch her something connected with putting curses on recalcitrant mothers. She rose to the surface in an instant but her lovely, bright, blue eyes were flashing defiance.

"I rather fancy someone's beaten you to it," said Mefin when the mermaid came up to the surface once more. "She's a bit of one of those already."

"She is peuh! If she will not let you marry me," said the mermaid who was getting really rather cross by this time.

"Shall I have to dig a pond or something in the garden for you if we get married?" asked Mefin, ever thinking of the practical side of things and trying to recall if he had read anything in his tenancy agreement or the *Railway Rule Book* or the *Passenger Manual* about mermaids. "I don't think the railway company will like that."

"Do not be stupid, I cannot leave ze sea," said the mermaid, as if it were the most natural thing in the world, which it was to her. "Surely you know zat." Of course he did not know that but she was not to know that he did not know that. In truth she had not spoken to a mortal before. Her papa had warned her about talking to mortals but as we have already discovered her papa had warned her about taking directions from dolphins and she had not listened to him on that subject either. "I should not 'ave spent so long in ze rivier, but you are so 'ansome when I saw you walking over ze bridge I just 'ad to stay and talk to you. However I must go back to the sea tonight or I will die."

"Oh I say," said Mefin. "I shouldn't like you to die. Perhaps if you went back to the sea now I could come down on the train tomorrow to Aberaeron and we could have a chat there."

"It is very triste," said the mermaid, and a big salty tear ran down her cheek. "But eef I stay 'ere in ze rivier I will die. But 'eef I go back to the sea without you I weel die of ze broken 'eart. I weel start to sing my death song while you go and ask your mama eef you can marry me. Eet will save time later if she refuses so I weel 'ave time to put a curse on her before I die." And with that she set up a plaintive wail that resembled a rather gurgling rendition of 'Myfanwy' although the effect was a little spoilt by the chorus sounding distinctly like 'The Campbells are Coming'.

Mefin was hardly capable of running but he made all the speed he could back to the station master's house. He threw open the door to the living room and announced to his mother.

"Mother, I'm going to marry a mermaid I have met in the River Teifi. She hasn't any clothes on, a long green tail and the loveliest, loveliest face I ever saw in my whole life." He looked imploringly at his mother.

"Whatever," said his mother waving one hand in a generally dismissive air and popping a mentholated lozenge into her mouth with the other.

"But mother," said Mefin, "have you no objection to my marrying with a mermaid. I shall have to give up my post on the railway and go to live in the sea. I do not suppose I shall be able to live in Cardigan Bay for the water is much too cold. I shall have to move to the Mediterranean at least and I cannot commute from there. It means you will be unable to stay in the station master's house. I expect you should be able to come and live with us in the Mediterranean Sea, there's bound to be plenty of room, but I fear you shall not like your daughter-in-law. She is of a rather independent mind."

Mefin's mother placed another mentholated lozenge on her tongue, drew a ring of lipstick around one of her nipples and muttered, "whatever".

Pausing only to take the last two tins of sardines from the larder Mefin rushed back to the river bridge. There he could hear the mermaid singing 'The Campbells are Coming'. He came down to the river bank and called to her and she swam to the shallows.

"Mother says I may marry you," Mefin called over the darkening surface of the water.

"Vite, vite," called back the mermaid. "We 'ave a long way to go to the sea and I must be there before daybreak." Mefin started to wade into the water that was bitterly cold. The mermaid could not refrain from laughing. Then she blushed. "You cannot come in like zat," she called and turned her head away in embarrassment. "Oo ever 'eard of a merhomme in ze water wis clothings on. It ees very naughty and we are not married yet. You must save zat sort of sing for our wedding night. You naughty, naughty Welshman you. Quick get out of your clothings before all ze fishes are scandalized. Ah weel never live zis down."

"But the water is so cold," protested Mefin.

"Eet will not be cold wiz my arms around you and my nice warm tail up against you. Come, come my love. Zer is so leetle time."

And nor was the water cold with her perfect arms around him

and her beautiful, long, dark-brown hair flowing over him as she propelled him down the river at a speed that even his trains could not match. They shot through the falls at Cenarth where the coracle men all said there must be sturgeon back in the river because they saw a massive fish flying through the water, bigger than any salmon and heading for the sea. One man saw them both as they passed under the town bridge at Cardigan just before the dawn broke. They had come up for air and the mermaid had Mefin in her perfect arms and was cradling his limp head against her magnificent bosom and he saw them as plain as day but he was the town drunk and no one believed him and the mermaid swam on unperturbed.

The next morning they found Mefin's clothes on the banks of the stream, his bowler hat and his boots placed beside the neat pile with nothing missing except his whistle and it remains a mystery to this day why he should have thrown himself in the river and why they never found his body and for what reason of grief or guilt it was that he took his railway whistle with him.

There is another mystery of which they know nothing in Lampeter but it is said that off the coast of Marseille, when the express trains leave station, you can see a group of what looks like porpoises frisking in the blue waters as the sun goes down and there is always the sound of a railway whistle.

Les Chamberlain

WELSH
nicknames

The stories behind
our more unusual
nicknames

yLolfa

£3.95

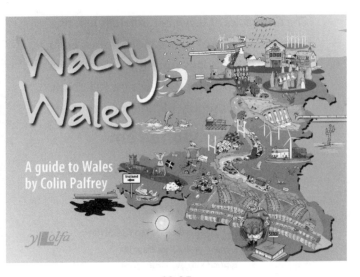

Wacky Wales

A guide to Wales
by Colin Palfrey

y Lolfa

£3.95

The Chronicles of Gwynfor Cornetti is just one of a whole range of publications from Y Lolfa. For a full list of books currently in print, send now for your free copy of our new full-colour catalogue. Or simply surf into our website

www.ylolfa.com

for secure on-line ordering.

TALYBONT CEREDIGION CYMRU SY24 5HE
e-mail ylolfa@ylolfa.com
website www.ylolfa.com
phone (01970) 832 304
fax 832 782